SUPERBASE 7

KADENA

SUPERBASE 7
KADENA
Shogun Warriors of the PACAF

Tony Holmes and Robbie Shaw

The authors would like to thank the men and women of the 313th Air Division and in particular Lieutenant Colonel Winkelmann, Lieutenant Colonel John Toner, Lieutenant Bob McCarty and Staff Sergeant Bobby Thomas of Air Force Public Relations. Thanks also to Colonel Lee Shelton and Lieutenant Colonel Frank Burns from the 9th SRW, Major Richard Smith from the 909th ARS, Captain Roger Burton from VMA-214, Thomas Gordon, and last, but by no means least, Randy Krumback of Flight Systems.

Published in 1989 by Osprey Publishing Limited
59 Grosvenor Street, London W1X 9DA

© Tony Holmes and Robbie Shaw 1989

British Library Cataloguing in Publication Data
Holmes, Tony
    Kadena: US airpower in the Pacific
    1. United States. Air Force. Military aircraft — Illustrations
    I. Title II. Shaw, Robbie III. Series
    623.74′.6′0973

    ISBN 0-85045-922-2

Editor Dennis Baldry
Designed by Paul Kime
Printed in Hong Kong

Front Cover Operating from an island in the Pacific does create some corrosion problems so a thorough shower awaits all returning aircraft at Kadena. This F-15C Eagle from the 67th Tactical Fighter Squadron (TFS) is actually using the shower facility on the US Navy ramp

Back Cover While the crew clamber about beneath the wing on their RF-4C, the squadron maintainers prepare to fire up the twin General Electric J79 turbojets. The operators of this recce-Phantom II are the 15th Tactical Reconnaisance Squadron (TRS), a unit with over 20 years' experience on the 'bent wing bird' from St Louis

Title pages Definitely one of the rarer aircraft at Kadena, the sinister SR-71A Blackbird still has the ability to turn the head of the crustiest line master sergeant. Assigned to the 9th Strategic Reconnaissance Wing based at Beale Air Force Base in California, Detachment One celebrated its twentieth anniversary at Kadena in March 1988. Two SR-71s and 325 men make up the detachment and they conduct their operations autonomously. As Lieutenant Colonel Frank Burns, logistics director for Det 1, put it: 'We are not part of the 313th or the 18th, or anything. We run our own show' (*Courtesy Toshiki Kudo*)

Right With the lush tropical vegetation of the hills around Okinawa as a backdrop, a pair of 18th TFW F-15C Eagles begin another routine patrol. Parked on the hard-standing in the foreground are two USAF aircraft from the opposite end of the performance spectrum. The WC-135B belongs to the 55th Weather Reconnaissance Sqn based at McClellan Air Force Base in California. This is one of six aircraft still performing the weather recce role, ten having been converted from the standard C-135B transport version in 1965. The overall glossy grey C-130H parked behind the WC-135B belongs to the 21st Tactical Air Sqn which is part of the 374th Tactical Air Wing stationed at Clark Air Force Base in the Philippines

Introduction

When viewed in the overall tactical scenario it is perhaps fitting that the majority of aircraft attached to the 313th Air Division proudly wear the historical symbol of power in the Orient; the mask of the 'Shogun'. After all, the 313th is the resident unit at Kadena Air Base, arguably the most important facility of the Pacific Air Forces.

The small Japanese island of Okinawa is the home of Kadena. The largest in the group of islands which form the Ryuku chain, Okinawa is only 65 miles long and varies in width from two to 17 miles. However, the combined military might of US Forces Pacific and the Japanese Self-Defence Force ensure that the island lives up to its nickname, 'The Keystone of the Pacific'. The largest of three units attached to the Yokota, Japan, based Fifth Air Force, the 313th Air Division also consists of three groups, all equally vital in performing the Division's mission effectively. The most obvious of these is the 18th Tactical Fighter Wing, the 'teeth' of Kadena. Three squadrons of McDonnell Douglas F-15Cs and a single unit of the older RF-4C Phantom II, make up the 18th TFW. The F-15Cs are tasked with the vital role of air superiority for the immediate region and as a force multiplier and 'political persuder' when forward deployed to bases in South Korea. The venerable RF-4s have been providing up-to-date photographic images of 'enemy' installations for the 18th TFW for over 21 years, with no immediate replacement appearing for this classic piece of 'heavy metal' from St Louis.

Keeping Kadena running smoothly is the responsibility of the 18th Combat Support Wing. The Wing has been based at Kadena since November 1954 and provides everything from base security police to chapel services. The third unit permanently based on Okinawa is the 400th Munitions Maintenance Sqn (Theater), the largest such squadron in the entire Air Force. Charged with the responsibility of maintaining 'a theater war reserve of material and conventional munitions as directed by Headquarters Pacific Air Command', the squadron also provides munitions support to the 18th TFW. The area occupied by the 400th MMS is as large again as Kadena Air Base proper, with more than 35,000 short tons of munitions valued at $350 million stored in the storage area.

Strategic Air Command also has a sizeable representation at Kadena, 21 KC-135 Stratotankers either on permanent detachment or on rotation from Stateside SAC units, usually occupying the northern side of the base. Two of the major customers which rely heavily on the venerable Boeing also belong to SAC. They are, of course, the E-3 Sentry and the SR-71 Blackbird, or 'Habu'. These aircraft are the 'eyes and ears' of the 313th Air Division, the importance of Kadena being shown once again by the fact that it was the first overseas location to operate 9th Strategic Reconnaissance Wing SR-71s on a permanent basis when Detachment One was established in March 1968. The lumbering giants of the Military Airlift Command complete the busy picture of Kadena's 'Aviation Team'. A constant stream of C-5 Galaxies and stretched C-141B Starlifters arrive and depart from the MAC complex with clockwork regularity.

All these separate units combine to form Kadena Air Base, a powerful protector on the rim of the Pacific. Just as the 'Shogun' was the supreme ruler throughout the islands for hundreds of years, so too will Kadena and its Air Wing continue to be a major force supporting allied and free-world nations in the area.

Contents

Right The 'No Gun Shoguns', one of a pair of specially marked RF-4Cs from the 15th Tactical Reconnaissance Sqn which participated in the biennial 'RAM' exercise, the premier contest for recce units worldwide

F-15 Eagle, 18th TFW

Above An 18th TFW pilot watches warily as he carefully manoeuvres his mount beneath a KC-135Q from the 909th Air Refuelling Sqn

Right The F-15C Eagle is a truly beautiful aircraft, the fighter wing at Kadena having flown this type since September 1979

Above Toting a single AIM-9 'Lima' on the port wing pylon, an F-15C from the 67th TFS tops up its tanks. With inflight refuelling the Eagle can stay on patrol for an incredible 15 hours, although the pilot's level of fatigue by this stage would be considerable

Right Having completed the JP-5 transaction the 67th TFS Eagle drifts back behind the KC-135 and prepares to resume its patrol

With both the lead and the wingman mounting 600 US gallon drop tanks on the fuselage centreline, these two F-15Cs from the 12th TFS are equipped in the standard patrol configuration

Left Parked in its 'flow through' shed at dusk, an F-15C from the 67th TFS is bathed in the last of the day's sunlight. Prominent in this view are the twin variable area afterburner nozzles which were originally covered with metal plates, known colloquially as 'turkey feathers.' These caused problems so they were removed, exposing the mechanics of the nozzles. Also visible in the extended position is the runway arrestor hook

Above Approximately 72 F-15s call Kadena Air Base home and theoretically each aircraft has a 'flow through' shed assigned to it

Left Devoid of all external stores, bar a single AIM-9L Sidewinder, this 67th TFS Eagle is probably about to undertake a brief proving flight after having some small mechanical fault rectified. These brief 'warranty check' flights usually entail the pilot putting the aircraft through its full flight parameters to ensure that everything is functioning at 100 per cent

Above Hardened shelters (HASs) are also being progressively made available to the 18th TFW. The majority of shelters are used to house the 15th TRS RF-4C Phantom IIs. Here a 12th TFS F-15 taxies past two opened shelters

Main picture Wearing the serial 78-544 this F-15C was the obvious choice when it came to selecting the Commanding Officer's aircraft for the third Eagle squadron at Kadena, the 44th TFS. All the F-15s at Kadena were drawn from the Fiscal Year 1978 production run

Inset Only one aircraft at Kadena wears all four squadron crests, and that is the F-15 of Colonel La Tourette, 18th TFW commander. The Wing first stood up in January 1927 as the 18th Pursuit Group and was stationed at Wheeler Field on the island of Oahu in Hawaii. The 18th was decimated on 7 December 1941, during the Japanese surprise attack on the Hawaiian islands. After extensive re-equipping and training the wing, now designated the 18th Fighter Group, moved to the South Pacific in March 1943 and operated from Guadalcanal, New Guinea and the Philippines. It finished the war flying P-38 Lightnings out of Mindanao. The unit remained in the Philippines until July 1950 when it moved to Korea. By this stage the 18th had been redesignated once again and now flew F-80 Shooting Stars and F-51 Mustangs in the fighter-bomber role. In early 1953 the group standardized on the F-86 Sabre. Once the conflict in Korea was over the 18th moved to Kadena and re-equipped with F-100 Super Sabres in 1957, the group being deactivated and the 18th Tactical Fighter Wing assuming direct control of the 12th, 44th and 67th Tactical Fighter Squadrons. The mighty F-105D Thunderchief arrived at Kadena in 1962 and two years later the wing started rotating aircraft and crews to South-east Asia to support the war effort in Vietnam. The squadrons transitioned onto the F-4 Phantom II in 1967, a marque the wing was to fly until 1979 when the new F-15C replaced the venerable fighter/bomber in all but one of the wing's squadrons

Left The bald eagle symbol of the 12th TFS

Above An entirely immaculate aircraft, Colonel La Tourette's F-15C is always kept in pristine condition. Unlike US Navy squadrons, where all aircraft are shared amongst the pilots, very rarely is the Wing CO's machine flown by anyone else. Just visible behind the F-15 is a Japanese Air Self-Defence Force Mitsubishi MU-2J

Right Sitting on the final check pad two F-15s from the 'Vampire Squadron', the 44th TFS, await final clearance before they begin their morning patrol. The 44th won the prestigious Hughes Trophy in 1982, the award being presented to the best air-to-air fighter squadron in the Air Force

Inset The familiar ZZ tail code of the 18th TFW. Originally only worn by aircraft of the 15th TRS, the wing asked Tactical Air Command in 1975 if all four squadrons could wear the code, a request which was duly approved

With its speed brake deployed, a 67th TFS Eagle taxies back to the flightline after completing a routine patrol. The large speed brake is formed mainly out of glassfibre honeycomb and is deployed by a single hydraulic jack. Unlike its predecessor, the F-4 Phantom II, the F-15 does not have a drag chute fitted (*Courtesy Toshiki Kudo*)

Above Military jet aircraft are noisy beasts and the F-15 is no exception. To appease the locals, but still allow the technicians to operate effectively, several engine test cells have been constructed at Kadena. Here a 67th TFS F-15D runs up, the immense noise of its Pratt & Whitney F100-PW-100 turbofans being effectively muffled within the cell

Right above Just prior to taxiing onto one of Kadena's two runways, an F-15D from the 12th TFS is given the 'once-over' by squadron maintenance men

Right below The pilot waits patiently while the brief visual checklist is performed beneath him. Various stencils and antennae plus the formation light strip can all be clearly seen

The standard F-15C canopy is a fighter pilot's dream, large, clear and giving
a totally unobstructed view. The twin-seat D model is even larger with the
canopy forming a perfect curve over the crew's heads

A maintenance man removes the safety pins on the launch rail and gives the ordnance a good tug. This ensures that it is securely attached to the wing pylon. Here an AIM-9L mounted to a 44th TFS machine is given the treatment

Above Partially obscured behind the instrument panel shroud and the canopy frame, an Eagle pilot mentally prepares himself for the forthcoming mission. He is wearing a lightweight HGU-55/P 'bone dome', the standard issue amongst F-15 pilots. The helmet helps reduce pilot fatigue when performing high G manoeuvres

Right A formation take-off for a pair of 67th TFS F-15C Eagles. The 67th was activated as a pursuit squadron in January 1941. The squadron initially flew from bases in northern Australia in the first months of the war and eventually fought its way through to the Philippines. The 'Fighting Cocks' accrued more combat experience in both Korea and Vietnam, acting as pioneering 'Wild Weasel' drivers in the latter conflict using F-4Cs. More recently the 67th was the first squadron in the Pacific Air Forces to acquire the F-15, an aircraft they have used effectively, winning the Hughes Trophy in 1983 and 1986

Left The variable intake ramps are fully lowered as a pair of 12th TFS F-15s roar away from Kadena Air Base. The gap between the two Eagles is self-evident! (*Courtesy USAF*)

Above Moments away from full gear retraction this F-15 will soon be climbing to operational height. Using full afterburner the F-15 has an initial rate of climb of an incredible 50,000 feet a minute

Main picture As if attached to the wing of the KC-135 itself, 12th TFS F-15s await their turn to break formation and pull in behind the Stratotanker for refuelling. Once replenished the pilot drops back and then formates on the starboard wing of the tanker

Inset Flying a formation much tighter than normal for photographic purposes, three 12th TFS F-15s cruise over the fluffy stratocumulus which covers the Pacific ocean below

With downtown Okinawa just visible through the murk below, two 12th TFS F-15s run over the airfield and 'pitch out' one after the other. Just like naval aviators, Air Force pilots take pride in their tight break and bank ability, a routine performed after every mission. Because of the high humidity which encompasses Okinawa virtually all year round spectacular contrails stream off the aircraft as they pull high Gs over the base

Above The aircraft break right in a slow echelon turn away from the KC-135 and will soon be back on station to resume the patrol. The large wing area of the F-15 can be seen from this view as well as the diagonally clipped wingtips which help alleviate buffet and wing loading problems

Right A considerable amount of maintenance work is carried out on 18th TFW aircraft after dusk because they are usually needed first thing the following morning. The night also brings a degree of coolness for the hard-working flight line crews

RF-4C Phantom II, 15th TRS

Two 15th TRS RF-4Cs sit on the hard-standing outside their respective hardened shelters. The Phantom in the foreground is 68-582 which, along with 68-551, participated in 'RAM 86'

Left Having dropped off its brake parachute (hence the opening of the tailcone door) a 'Cotton Pickers' recce-Phantom taxies back to its HAS

Above The large slab fin of the Phantom has seen some colourful markings over the years but unfortunately the 15th TRS are quite subdued in comparison. This particular RF-4C was one of 21 aircraft which made up Block 33 from the St Louis plant in 1966/67

Above left The 18th TFW insignia reflects the wing's motto *Unguibus et Rostro*, 'With Talons and Beak', and all aircraft assigned wear the 'fighting cock' on the left intake

Above right Originally formed as the 2nd Aviation School Sqn in May 1917, the unit was soon redesignated the 15th Aero Sqn and assigned a complement of Curtiss JN-4 Jenny and de Havilland DH-4 Flying Coffin aircraft. Between the wars the 15th became an observation squadron. Equipped with P-51 Mustangs the 'Cotton Pickers' flew extensively throughout occupied Europe during the Second World War as part of the 67th Observation Group. The squadron also took part in the Korean conflict where they flew long range photo reconnaissance strikes into MiG Alley and along the Yalu River in RF-86F Sabres. The 15th TRS moved to Yokota in 1955 and replaced its Sabres with the Thunderflash. Kadena became home for the squadron the following year and the Voodoo replaced the RF-84 in 1958. The unit took its Voodoos to Vietnam in 1964 as part of the 2nd Air Division's 15th Reconnaissance Task Force. The war-weary RF-101s gave way to the brand new RF-4C Phantom II in 1967, an aircraft still associated with the 15th TRS today

Right USAF Phantoms are not often seen with their outer wing panels – a legacy of the F-4's naval parentage – folded. This aircraft, a Block 31 RF-4C, also has its flare compartment doors open revealing the dispenser tubes for the night photography aids. There is a flare compartment on either side of the tail fin

Above The 'Shogun Warrior' and the 18th TFW 'Cock' adorn the port intake of all 15th TRS RF-4Cs

Right After every mission each 18th TFW aircraft taxies over one of several high pressure fresh water showers built into the ramps at Kadena. This simple but effective procedure helps keep the problem of corrosion in check. This particular Phantom is heavily loaded with two 370 gallon wing tanks, a 600 gallon centreline tank and an AN/ALQ101 ECM pod (*Courtesy Toshiki Kudo*)

Left The final checks are made by the ground crew on an RF-4 equipped with an AN/ALQ101 electronic countermeasures pod. The 15th TRS is the sole recce unit in the Pacific Air Forces and has a permanent detachment based at Osan in South Korea. Depot-level maintenance is carried out by Korean Air Lines at Kimhae

Above Standing astride his 'front office' Captain Knight checks the drogue parachute shackle at the top of the Martin-Baker Mk H7 ejector seat. A well-used Phantom, note the heavy weathering around the access panel and the splitter plate, the machine was about to undertake a proving flight. Perhaps that's why the pilot was checking his 'hot seat'!

Above The 15th TRS may be the only USAF RF-4 unit in the Pacific but occasionally their numbers are temporarily bolstered by transient visitors on the navy ramp. This RF-4B belongs to Marine Tactical Reconnaissance Squadron (VMFP) 3, and forms part of a permanent detachment forward deployed to Marine Corp Air Station Iwakuni, Japan, from their home base at MCAS El Toro, California. This particular Phantom was returning home from Thailand when 'something broke', as the youthful crew put it, resulting in a diversion to Kadena for repairs

Left Draped over the port fuel tank the crew's G webbing contrasts markedly with the pale powdery grey of the VMFP-3 Phantom. The long slender antenna fitted to the intake is the radar homing and warning (RHAW) gear, a modification made to all navy and marine Phantoms following the lessons learnt in Vietnam. Nicknamed 'The Specters' or 'The Eyes of the Corps', VMFP-3 are the only unit equipped with the RF-4B and were formed at MCAS El Toro in July 1975. The squadron has a strength of about 25 to 30 aircraft, the survivors of 46 F-4Bs converted to the photo-recce role in 1965. Although progressively modernized over the ensuing 24 years the RF-4B, like its USAF cousin, is decidedly aged and in desperate need of a replacement. Just ask the crew of this weary Phantom

Main picture Two other F-4 Phantom IIs are present at Kadena although their flying days are definitely over. Both aircraft are F-4Cs, this one eventually to be displayed near gate two alongside other historical USAF aircraft. Although wearing the colours of the 199th Fighter Sqn, 154th Fighter Group, Hawaii Air National Guard, the Phantom flew with the 67th FIS from 1968 to August 1979 when it was transferred to the Guard. Base historian, Thomas Gordon, hopes to have the aircraft resprayed in its original South-east Asian scheme

Inset A relatively new scheme to Kadena; only four or five 15th TRS RF-4s are painted in the two-tone grey 'Egyptian One' colours. Generally not a popular scheme with the crews because most squadron missions are flown 'down in the weeds' where the old 'European One' colours were perfect, all RF-4s will eventually be painted up like 72-155. This particular Phantom was the second last RF-4C built, one of four in the Block 53 batch

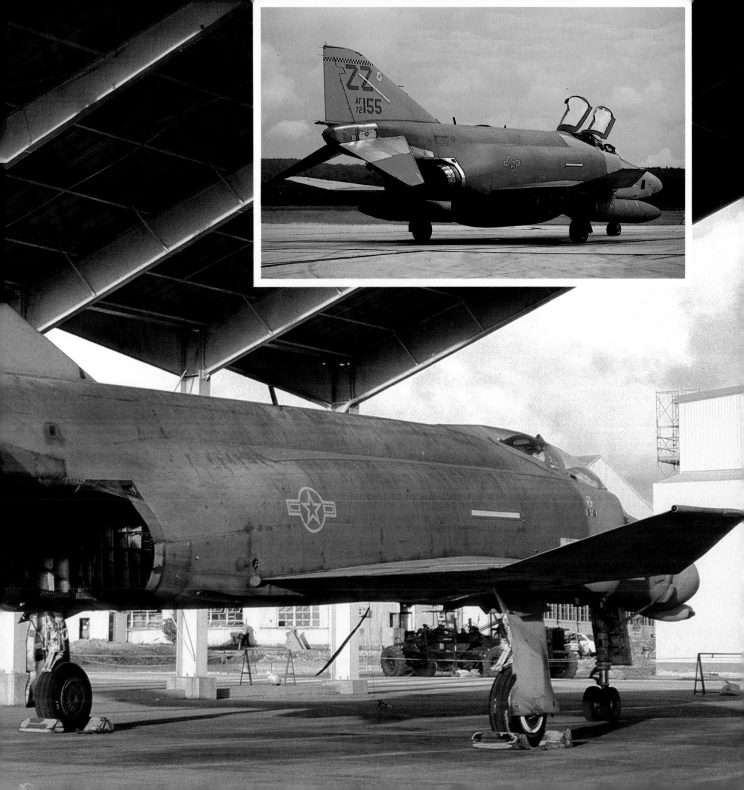

E-3A, 961st AWACS

Right Framed by the flying boom and ruddervators, an E-3C Sentry of the 961st Airborne Warning and Control Sqn slowly edges forward to be refuelled. About halfway along the fuselage can be seen a new smaller rotating radome

This page Another mission is completed as an E-3A touches down after a long patrol. Behind the 961st AWACS machine is the navy ramp, a solitary P-3 and assorted Marine Corps A-4s and F-4s dispersed there

Above The colourful unit badges of the AWACS detachment at Kadena. The 961st are the solitary E-3 squadron in the Pacific Air Forces, three aircraft and about 392 operations and maintenance personnel permanently assigned to the unit. Like all Sentry squadrons the 961st is part of the 552nd AWAC Wing which is in turn controlled by the 28th Air Division at Tinker Air Force Base in Oklahoma

Right With the huge radome housing the Westinghouse APY-1 radar forming an impressive backdrop, the maintenance crew go about the final stages of an engine change which took a record two hours to complete. The usual time taken to swap a Pratt & Whitney TF33-100 is about ten hours

Overleaf The 961st AWACS was originally activated in December 1954, the majestic EC-121 Constellation being the unit's first mount. After flying the 'Connie' for 15 years the squadron was deactivated, being reformed ten years later at Kadena Air Base. This E-3A is bathed in floodlights on the joint TAC/SAC ramp at Kadena

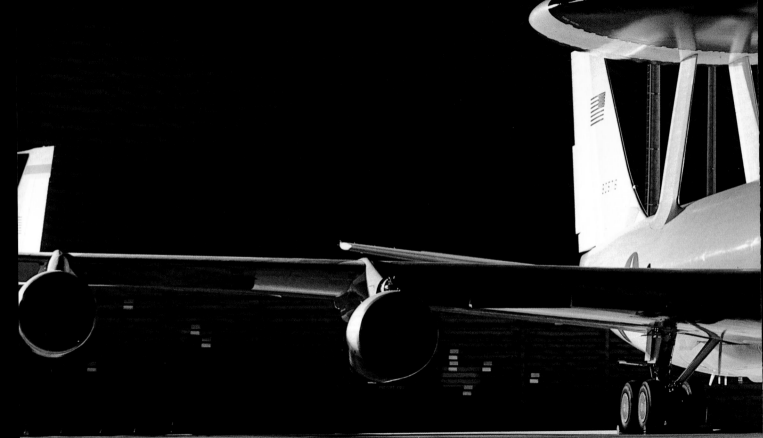

RC-135, 55th SRW

One of the more clandestine aircraft which occasionally calls Kadena home is the Boeing RC-135. This particular aircraft, an RC-135V, is attached to the 55th Strategic Reconnaissance Wing based at Offutt AFB, Nebraska. Originally built in 1963 as a standard KC-135B the aircraft was converted into an RC-135C and has been progressively updated through the 'C' and 'U' marks to its present designation. The most distinguishing features of the RC-135V are the large cheek fairings either side of the nose which house the sideways-looking airborne radar (SLAR), and the small forest of blade and plate aerials under the fuselage which form an integral part of the Sigint system

KC-135 Stratotanker

Left Moments away from touching down, a 909th Air Refuelling Squadron KC-135A glides into Kadena after completing yet another refuelling mission

Below The tail markings on the 909th KC-135s leave you in no doubt as to where they are based. The unit is part of the 376th Strategic Wing and is the only refuelling squadron permanently based out of the United States

This particular KC-135 was delivered to the Air Force in 1959 but as with most of SAC's tanker fleet this aircraft looks absolutely superb. The aircraft recently went through the 'Shiny Eagle' programme which entails stripping the airframe down to component stage and rebuilding it. The last new KC-135 was delivered to the USAF in January 1965

Above Devoid of the distinctive blue, red and white 'Kadena' marking on the fin-tip, this KC-135A has only recently been assigned to the 909th. The aircraft is undergoing a full technical inspection before joining the 17 other KC-135s which make up the squadron. The various colours painted on the extended boom help both the pilot and the boom operator calculate the distance between the tanker and the recipient. The 'cherry-picker' Ford truck is being used as a platform by the ground crew to adorn the aircraft's fin with the squadron colours

Right All the 909th ARS KC-135s wear this stylized black radome which is outlined in white and is continued on behind the windscreen panels. The fuel system in the KC-135A is made up of 21 tanks, 12 in the wing and nine in the fuselage, allowing the tanker to carry 31,200 US gallons of fuel

C-9B Skytrain II

Regular visitors to Kadena are the C-9B Skytrain IIs of VR-59, one of the US Navy's fleet logistics squadrons. The navy received a total of 19 Skytrain IIs and they are comparable to the civilian DC-9 series 30 and 40

C-130E/HC-130P

Below The workhorse of the USAF. Military Airlift Command C-130 Hercules transports regularly fly into Kadena from bases throughout Asia. This C-130E belongs to the 345th Tactical Airlift Squadron, part of the 316th Tactical Air Group

Right Fitted with the Fulton recovery system 'thimble' nose but devoid of the forks and guard lines which also form part of the rescue package, this HC-130P belongs to the Kadena based 33rd Aerospace Rescue and Recovery Squadron. The dorsal fairing houses the Cook Electric Company advanced directional finding equipment. The 33rd ARRS commands the Western Pacific Rescue Co-ordination Centre (WESTPAC RCC) which provides a 24-hour rescue capability. Since it was established in 1974 the WESTPAC RCC has participated in saving more than 2100 lives. Two other rescue squadrons, the 31st ARRS at Clark AFB in the Philippines and the 38th ARRS at Osan AFB in South Korea, also support the WESTPAC RCC

C-12/UC-12B

Left MAC C-12s of the 13th Military Airlift Squadron Det 2 are the only permanent command unit based at Kadena, although the 603rd Military Airlift Support Group handles a constant stream of C-5s, C-141s and C-130s, plus Flying Tigers' 747s on charter. This is one of two C-12Fs which make up the Kadena detachment, with Det 1 and Det 3 based at Clark and Osan respectively. All three Dets are parented by the 374th Tactical Air Wing based at Clark AFB

Below The high- and low-visibility C-12 markings. In the foreground is a Kadena based C-12F of the 13th MAS and parked alongside it is a US Army C-12A from the little-known Corps of Engineers unit. The C-12A is the utility/light transport version of the Beech Super King Air

Right Wearing the distinctive Marine Corps colours of scarlet and gold, a locally based UC-12B from MCAS Futenma comes in on finals to Kadena. Corps aviation is highly visible in the skies over Okinawa (*Courtesy Toshiki Kudo*)

Above Quite a way from home, this US Navy UC-12B is based at Naval Air Station Atsugi, the home of Carrier Air Wing Five, situated about 40 miles southwest of Tokyo. The only permanent naval aircraft attached to Naval Air Facility Kadena is the UC-12B of the Commander Fleet Activities Okinawa

C-141B Starlifter

Right Wearing what looks like a freshly sprayed on 'European One' scheme, a C-141B motors out past 'Habu Hill' with its taxiing lights blazing. This particular Starlifter belongs to the 63rd Military Airlift Wing, based at Norton AFB in California

Below The old and the new. Although both these Starlifters are B models, the one in the foreground still wears the now superseded MAC light grey and white with black trim scheme worn by the C-141 for almost twenty years. Both these aircraft belong to the 60th Military Airlift Wing, the only unit to fly the C-141 in the colours of the Military Air Transport Service back in 1965 when it was designated the 1501st Air Transport Wing. The 60th is based at Travis AFB, California

Left The considerable wing anhedral and the closely grouped Pratt &
Whitney TF33-P-7 turbofans are two of the distinguishing features of the
C-141. A total of 284 C-141As were originally built by Lockheed of which 270
were stretched between 1978 and 1982. This modification gave MAC extra
lifting power equivalent to 90 extra C-141As. Having been refuelled by six
Mack tankers a C-141B of the 60th MAW taxies out to the runway to
commence another long, laborious flight

Above The 'Stars and Bars' show out prominently against the tactical 'lizard'
scheme which totally covers this 63rd MAW C-141B. The Universal Aerial
Refuelling Slipway Installation mounted on top of the forward fuselage was
also added to the Starlifter fleet during the lengthening conversion

C-5A, 60th MAW

Right Regular visitors to the 603rd Military Airlift Support Group facility at Kadena are the C-5 Galaxies of the 60th MAW. The amount of wingtip clearance the C-5s have over the small hills surrounding the taxiways at Kadena isn't a lot! To give the Galaxy more 'bite' into the air when it takes off and lands huge leading edge slats are deployed, as can be seen here

Below Although the C-5 has been overshadowed somewhat lately by the huge Antonov An-124 Ruslan, the Galaxy is still a very impressive aircraft. This 60th MAW C-5A wears the standard 'European One' scheme which gives the aircraft a very sinister appearance but also creates internal heat problems, especially in the Pacific

Inset Forming an impressive backdrop for two rare visitors to Kadena, a C-5A of the 60th MAW basks in the afternoon sun. The glossy UH-1H Huey belongs to the United States Army Japan VIP transport unit, whilst the Kawasaki C-1A is a 401st *Hikotai* machine of the Japanese Air Self-Defence Force

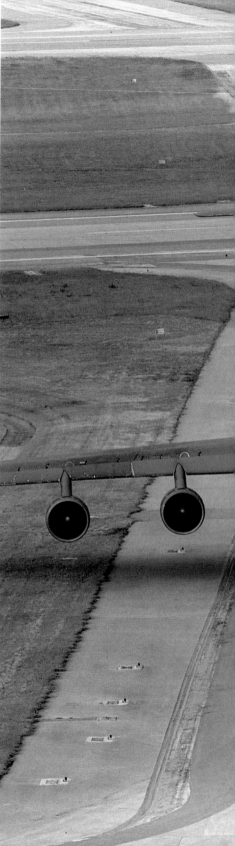

Japanese Air Self-Defence Force

Left Designed and built totally within Japan, the Kawasaki C-1 was the result of a specification drawn up by the Air Self-Defence Force for a replacement for the Curtiss C-46 Commando. A total of 31 C-1s were built and they equip three *hikotais*, each the Japanese equivalent of a squadron

Below The 401st *Hikotai* is part of the Air Transport Wing based at Komaki on mainland Japan. The 401st is currently phasing out it's C-1s and replacing them with the C-130H Hercules, the Kawasakis going to the 403rd *Hikotai*

An aircraft which will never win prizes for its good looks, but one which has served faithfully in the surface air rescue role for over a decade, is the Shin Meiwa US-1. Based on the ASW capable PS-1, the US-1 is fully amphibious, 11 having been built for the Fleet Air Force. This particular aircraft was the fifth one built and was delivered to the Fleet in 1981. It belongs to the 31st *Kokugun* (Wing) and is operated alongside seven other US-1s by the 71st *Kokutai* at Naval Air Station Iwakuni

Left Deployed to Okinawa for the annual 'Kadena Karnival', this Mitsubishi T-2 belongs to the 6th *Hikotai* at Tsuiki. The 6th is a fighter squadron which operates the single-seat Mitsubishi F-1, but like USAF fighter units, two or three two-seat T-2's are on strength also. Mounted on both inner stores pylons are two 220 US gallon drop tanks fitted for the long trip to Kadena

Above The Mitsubishi F-1/T-2 series is powered by two Ishikawajima–Harima TF40 engines which are licensed copies of the Rolls-Royce/Turboméca Adour turbofan. Like the F-15B/D, the T-2 is fully combat capable, mounting a 20 mm JM-61 rotary-barrel cannon in the portside fuselage, Mitsubishi Electric radar (J/AWG-12) and full wiring and mountings for AIM-9B Sidewinder missiles. The extra seat does however result in the T-2 lacking the Ferranti 6TNJ-F inertial navigation system, the APR-3 radar homing and warning system computer, and the ASQ-1 weapons release computer. The 6th *Kokutai* was the last squadron to transition onto the F-1 when it replaced the well used F-86F in 1980

The Stallion

Left A fairly common sight in the skies over Kadena are the CH-53s of the 1st Marine Aircraft Wing, Fleet Marine Force Pacific, based at Marine Corps Air Station Futenma. This particular CH-53D belongs to Marine Heavy Helicopter (HMH) Sqn 462 based at MCAS Tustin in central California. Squadrons are periodically deployed to Futenma from Tustin

Above With its huge seven-blade main rotor head ripping into the moist tropical air, a CH-53E from Helicopter Combat Support Squadron (VC) 5 taxies onto the MAC terminal ramp. The US Navy operates about 30 CH-53Es, with VC-5 being based at NAS Cubi Point in the Philippines. Tasked with supporting aircraft carriers and air capable vessels of the Third and Seventh Fleets, these large helicopters range all over the Pacific and Indian Oceans

HH-3E Jolly Green Giant

A real combat seasoned veteran in the true sense of the word, the HH-3E Jolly Green Giant has seen over twenty years' service. These vital rescue helicoptors sport beefed-up armour and self-sealing tanks, modifications indicative of the Jolly Green Giant's hazardous 'down-in-the-weeds' role. Sitting up on jacks undergoing routine maintenance, this HH-3E belongs to the 33rd Aerospace Rescue and Recovery Sqn. All USAF Jolly Greens are due to be replaced by the Sikorsky HH-60A Night Hawk by the mid-1990s

VIP Aviation Detachment

Inset Assigned to Nine Corps and based at Camp Zama this is one of two UH-1H Hueys assigned to the United States Army Japan VIP Aviation Detachment. The Mount Fuji silhouette forms an integral part of this unit's badge and it can be seen on the pilot's door.

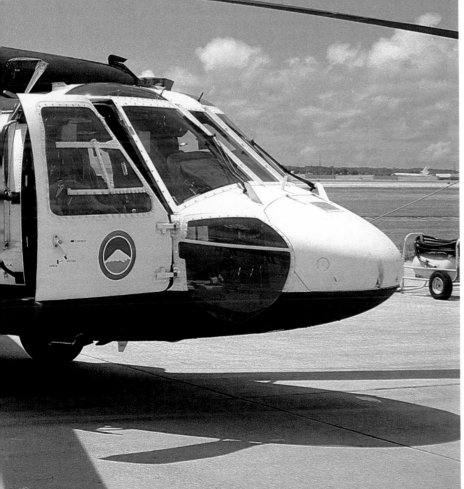

Main picture The VIP flight also operates three UH-60A Black Hawks alongside the UH-1s. Three UH-60s were delivered to Nine Corps in February 1986 and they offer a significant improvement in performance over the older Huey

OV-10A Bronco

Left 'We Control Violence'. A more apt squadron motto could not have been found to describe the role of the 19th Tactical Air Support Squadron! Equipped with 17 OV-10A Broncos the 19th is attached to the 5th Tactical Air Control Group and is based at Osan in South Korea. The 19th provides forward air control for both US and Korean Air Force attack aircraft

Below The high shoulder-mounted wing and twin boom arrangement give the OV-10 an incredibly short take-off run of just 740 feet. The 19th TASS flew OA-37B Dragonflies for some time before passing them onto the Koreans and re-equipping with the Bronco. The OA-10 Thunderbolt II has been mooted as a replacement for the OV-10 at Osan AFB sometime in the future

P-3C Orion

Right Although the US Navy's presence at Kadena has been scaled down significantly over the past ten years, a permanent detachment of P-3 Orions usually occupies a fair portion of the navy flight line. Home-based at Naval Air Station Moffett Field in California, Patrol Squadron (VP) 19 regularly forward deploys to NAF Kadena. Reserve Patrol Wing Pacific squadrons also call Kadena home occasionally (*Courtesy Toshiki Kudo*)

Below Totally devoid of the once distinct tail markings, a VP-40 P-3C Update III Orion sits innocuously on a damp flightline at dawn. VP-40 were the first patrol squadron to receive the 'new' Orions in 1985, the Update III variant having a new acoustic processor, new sonobuoy receiver, new auxiliary power unit and environmental-control systems added to the standard P-3C airframe

A-4 Skyhawk

Left Arguably one of the most famous, if not the most notorious of squadrons ever to take to the skies, Marine Attack Squadron 214 sometimes shares the navy side of Kadena with the P-3s. The various lumps and bumps affixed to the nose of this 'Blacksheep' A-4M provide essential target information to the pilot as well as blocking enemy radar which may be tracking the Skyhawk

Below Regularly deployed to Japan from their home base at MCAS Yuma, California, VMA-214 spent four months at Kadena in 1988 because of a flight line closure at MCAS Iwakuni. The 'Blacksheep' have been flying 'Heinemann's Hotrod' since January 1962 and are now one of only three frontline A-4M squadrons left in the Marine Corps

Above Initially formed in 1942, the 'Blacksheep' legend was built around a group of 27 pilots who found themselves 'squadronless' in the Pacific. Brought together under the leadership of Major Gregory 'Pappy' Boyington, the motley crew raked up a score of 197 Japanese planes destroyed or damaged in just 84 days, flying F-4U Corsairs. The squadron also saw combat in Korea and Vietnam

Right Wearing the initial low-visibility colour scheme first seen in 1981, a VMA-331 'Bumblebees' A-4M taxies in with its leading edge slats and wing spoilers deployed. The 'Bumblebees' now fly AV-8B Harrier IIs out of MCAS Cherry Point in North Carolina (*Courtesy Toshiki Kudo*)

Inset The 'Blacksheep' have over 30 A-4Ms on strength, many being ex-VMA-311 'Tomcats' aircraft left at Iwakuni for VMA-214 when the former unit returned to MCAS Yuma, Arizona, to begin transitioning onto the AV-8B. This A-4M is parked in the Marine Aircraft Group (MAG) 12 hangar at Kadena. Note the unusual angle of the all-moving tailplane and the deployed split trailing edge flaps and tailhook

Main picture A pair of A-4Ms from VMA-211, the rather flamboyantly named 'Wake Island Avengers', taxi out to begin the next stage in their 'cross-country' back to MCAS Iwakuni. Mounted on the centreline of each Skyhawk is a 150 US gallon droptank which helps to extend the rather short range of the aircraft on long flights (*Courtesy Toshiki Kudo*)

Left A VMA-214 A-4M in the old grey and white scheme departs on a mission. With the large ECM hump mounted on the fuselage spine immediately behind the pilot, rearward vision in the 'Mike' model A-4 is not brilliant (*Courtesy Toshiki Kudo*)

Above One of the rarer models in the Skyhawk family is the OA-4M, a dedicated forward air control (FAC) platform of which only 30 were constructed. Although equipped with the same electronics and ECM suite as the A-4M, the aircraft is powered by the lower rated Pratt & Whitney J52-P-8 engine instead of the more gutsy P-408 version as mounted in the single-seater. Assigned to Headquarters and Maintenance Squadron (H and MS) 12, 'Outlaws', based at MCAS Iwakuni, this OA-4M was providing FAC for VMA-214. Eight OA-4s equip H and MS 12 and they all wear a dark grey 'Yosemite Sam' cartoon character on the fin. The squadron has gained extensive combat experience over the years starting in the Pacific during the Second World War, continuing through Korea in the early 1950s, and finally flying the TF-9J Cougar in the skies over Vietnam

Inset The Marine Corps has five operational Intruder squadrons on strength and one training unit. This VMA(AW)-322 A-6E is based at MCAS Cherry Point in North Carolina. Built in the mid-1960s, this Intruder started life as an A-6A before being upgraded to its present A-6E TRAM standard

A-6E TRAM Intruder

Left The navy ramp at Kadena is a very popular spot with transient aircraft, particularly Corps machines. This A-6E (TRAM) belongs to VMA(AW)-242, 'The Batmen', forward deployed to the 1st Marine Air Wing at MCAS Iwakuni from MCAS El Toro, California. The Intruder is in fact being flown by the head 'Batman' himself, the VMA(AW)-242 Squadron CO! (*Courtesy Toshiki Kudo*)

Below Probably wishing they were somewhere else at the time, the crew of a VMA(AW)-332 'Polkadots' A-6E wait forlornly as the groundcrew try to trace a sudden fluid leak from one of the Pratt & Witney J52-P-8B turbofans which appeared moments before engine fire-up

A-7E Corsair II

Left Regular callers at NAF Kadena are aircraft from Carrier Air Wing (CVW) Five, the group attached to the venerable USS *Midway*. One squadron that won't be calling at Kadena again though is VA-56. Nicknamed the 'Champions', this squadron, along with sister-unit VA-93 'Ravens', was decommissioned in late 1986 when the air wing began the transition onto the F/A-18 Hornet. This particular A-7E is wearing the semi toned down overall gloss pearl grey scheme seen on Corsairs briefly in 1982/83 (*Courtesy Toshiki Kudo*)

Below One of the squadrons which replaced VA-56 onboard the USS *Midway* was VA-192, redesignated VFA-192 and now flying the F/A-18. A long term operator of the A-7E, VFA-192 was 'carrierless' when this photo was taken, nominally assigned to CVW-19 and the USS *Kitty Hawk* which was in fact in refit. Flamboyantly titled the 'World Famous Golden Dragons', VFA-192 earned notoriety as William Holden's squadron in the movie 'The Bridges at Toko Ri' (*Courtesy Toshiki Kudo*)

One of the 'new generation' aircraft now operated by the Marine Corps is the F/A-18A Hornet. This brand new Hornet belongs to VMFA-115 'Silver Eagles', the unit having the distinction of being the first F/A-18 equipped squadron to forward deploy to MCAS Iwakuni. Usually based at MCAS Beaufort, South Carolina, VMFA-115 deployed as part of Marine Air Group (MAG) 15 which is one of three groups under the command of Marine Air Wing One (*Courtesy Toshiki Kudo*)

F/A-18 Hornet

Overleaf Belonging to a squadron
with a long and distinguished
history, this brand new F/A-18A
basks in the mid-afternoon sun.
VMFA-122 was commissioned in
March 1942 on the F4F Wildcat, an
aircraft which the squadron flew in
combat over the New Hebrides
Islands. Midway through 1943
VMFA-122 converted onto the F4U-1
Corsair and continued to fly the
formidable Vought until 1947 when
the squadron had the distinction of
becoming the first jet unit in the
Corps when they received the FH-1
Phantom. Not an entirely successful
aircraft, the FH-1 soon gave way to
the markedly better F9F-5 Panther
and then in 1954 to the FJ-2 Fury.
Three years later VMFA-122
became the fastest squadron in the
Marine Corps when they traded in
their Furies for F-8A Crusaders.
Always at the forefront of Corps
aviation the squadron soon
transitioned onto the more capable
F-8E version of the Crusader. Then
began an association with a
legendary aircraft which was to last
20 years. The aircraft was of course
the F-4 Phantom II. Blooded on the
type in Vietnam, VMFA-122 finally
retired their F-4s in 1985 when they
converted onto the F/A-18

F-5E Tiger II, 26th Aggressor Squadron

Below Aside from the SR-71, the diminutive F-5E is arguably the most impressive aircraft on take-off at Kadena. Departing usually in pairs with their noses cranked up high due to the extendible forward gear leg, the Tiger IIs don't hang about as all take-offs are performed in afterburner. Wearing a scheme reminiscent of the F-5A 'Skoshi Tiger' days in Vietnam 20 years before, an F-5E of the 26th AS taxies out on another ACM mission

Left An impressive stack of 26th AS F-5Es. The squadron is based at Clark AFB in the Philippines and is attached to the 3rd Tactical Fighter Wing. Also assigned to the 3rd TFW is the 3rd TFS equipped with the F-4E and the 90th TFS which flies a mixed bag of F-4Es and 'Wild Weasel' F-4Gs. The two-digit nose code is taken from the last two numbers in the aircraft's serial

Left Although not based at Kadena the F-5Es of the 26th Aggressor Squadron spend a considerable period of time each year deployed there. Having just completed a long 'cross-country' ('cross-ocean' would be more appropriate!) to participate in the annual 'Kadena Karnival', this F-5 is about to undergo a post-flight check. The F-5E mounts a pair of M-39A2 revolver type 20 mm cannon in it's very slender nose

Above The F-5E does not possess a huge range simply because the small dimensions of the airframe allow only a modicum of fuel to be carried internally. For long flights the solution is to plumb the aircraft to a large 275 US gallon centreline fuel tank as has happened to this 26th AS F-5

Above 'TOPGUN' USAF style! Kitted out in the full regalia, including Ray-Ban sunnies, Major 'Wralph' Collins strikes the stereotypical 'fighter jock' pose in front of his 'office'. The visor protection cover is a real work of art

Left Powered by a pair of General Electric J85-GE-21 engines grouped snugly beneath a slab-sided tail fin, the F-5E is proof that simplicity in design can sometimes produce the best aircraft. The skilled cadre of pilots in the 26th AS quite often get the jump on their colleagues who are flying an aircraft worth about four times as much as their own.

CL-13 Sabre, Flight Systems Inc

Left An eternal classic, the Canadair CL-13 Sabre Mk 6 still graces the flightline at Kadena, albeit in civilian hands. Based in the Mojave Desert in California, Flight Systems Incorporated have fulfulled the target towing duties at Kadena since June 1982

Below Three Sabres are on strength at Flight Systems and these aircraft regularly deploy to other US Air Force Pacific bases such as Misawa in northern Japan and Osan and Taegu in South Korea

Opposite above A total of eight personnel run the Kadena detachment of Flight Systems; three pilots and five maintenance men. All the pilots are retired USAF fighter 'jocks' and their mounts are ex-Canadian and South African Air Force Sabres which were all built in 1954. Since 1982 the three aircraft have flown over 4000 sorties, averaging 800 a year or three to four per day. The Sabres are completely stripped and broken down to components every three years and Flight Systems is currently looking at re-engining the aircraft sometime in the future with Rolls-Royce Speys

Opposite below Fitted usually on the port hardpoint of the Sabres is the RMU-10/A reel pod, the aircraft balanced by a standard drop tank under the starboard wing. The TDU-10B target is attached to the pylon adjacent to the side of the pod

Above The target itself is quite a considerable size and only just fits under the Sabre's low wing. The target can be trailed up to 5000 feet behind the towing aircraft. Both the pod and the target combined are designated the A37U Target Tow System

Voodoo: before and after

Looking absolutely resplendent in its overall Air Defence Command blue/grey, this F-101B Voodoo flew into Kadena in 1986 as a battle damage repair aircraft

Left Two years later and the former pride and joy of the Oregon Air National Guard looks fit only for a local scrapyard. Based at the Portland International Airport, the F-101B was assigned to the 123rd Fighter Interceptor Squadron and was one of three units which formed the 142nd Fighter Interceptor Group

Above The mighty Voodoo called Kadena home for ten years during the 1950s and 1960s when the 15th Tactical Reconnaissance Squadron flew the RF-101. The Oregon Air National Guard traded in their weary F-101Bs in 1980 for slightly less weary F-4Cs. The unit is soon to transition onto the F-15A

Gate Guardians

Left The oldest of four aircraft displayed near gate two at Kadena is this North American F-86F Sabre painted in the colours of the 67th Fighter/Bomber Squadron. The 'Fighting Cocks' traded in their clapped-out F-51 Mustangs in February 1953 while the squadron was fighting in Korea. The Sabre is painted in the colours the 67th wore while based at Osan-ni in Korea

Below An aircraft of enormous historical importance exhibited alongside the F-86 is this camouflaged Super Sabre. Although painted up (incorrectly) to represent an 18th TFW F-100D the aircraft is in fact one of the original 203 F-100As initially built for the USAF. Spuriously serialled AF52-612, the aircraft is on long-term loan from the USAF Museum at Wright-Patterson AFB

Overleaf above Although travelling at a somewhat more sedate pace than it's immediate companions, this T-39A Sabreliner gave the USAF sterling service for many years as it plied endlessly between bases in the Pacific. Powered by a pair of small but noisy Garrett TFE731 turbofans, the T-39 utilized the wing of the F-86 Sabre, hence the name

Overleaf below Arguably the most impressive aircraft ever to grace the vast flightline at Kadena, the might Republic F-105 Thunderchief was based on Okinawa in the early 1960s. Over 70 'Thuds' were flown by the 18th TFW, replacing the F-100 in 1963. The 18th flew the F-105D from Korat Royal Thai Air Force Base over Vietnam from 1965 to 1967 before transitioning onto the F-4C Phantom II. This particular Thunderchief is painted in the natural silver scheme worn by the wing's 'Delta' model aircraft, but it is in fact an F-105F built in 1962